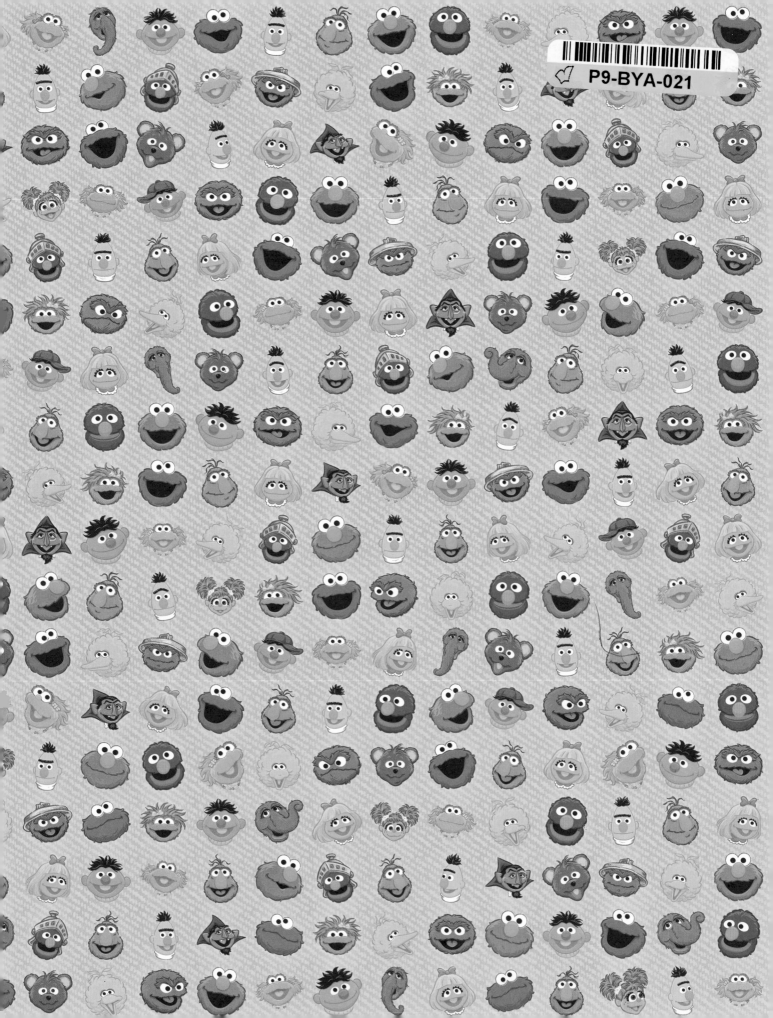

First published by Parragon in 2009

Parragon
Queen Street House
4 Queen Street
Bath BA1 1HE, UK

ISBN 978-1-4075-3809-9

Printed in China

123 SESAME STREET®

I L♥ve ARTS and Crafts

PaRragon

Bath · New York · Singapore · Hong Kong · Cologne · Delhi · Melbourne

CONTENTS

This book is full of creative, fun things to make for your family, your friends and yourself for all kinds of occasions.

TIPS FOR PARENTS AND CAREGIVERS

This book is for the whole family. Its primary purpose is to bring together parents and children, from preschoolers to teens, to have fun making things! True, making things with young children can take time and get a little messy. But it will be fun and it will give them a sense of achievement. Once children start making things, they just might become "crafters" for life.

The Importance of Doing Crafts with Children

The projects that appear in this book were designed for, worked on, and tested by young children and their families. Every craft project in this book highlights at least one task that a young child can perform. Make sure to choose projects with steps that you think your own child can accomplish with relative ease. Remember, what seems like a small, simple task to you—applying glue to the back of a piece of paper, coloring in a simple design, or arranging shells in a dish—is a big accomplishment for a small child, and can instill a sense of pride.

From the time a child picks up his first crayon until he reaches adulthood, he goes through several developmental stages with regard to arts and crafts—from scribbles (about age 2); to assigning meaning to shapes drawn (about age 5); to the creation of three-dimensional objects (about age 8.) Although the pace at which each child progresses may differ, important skills can be developed by working with crafts.

LEARNING SKILLS

- Logic, problem solving
- Basic math skills (measuring; using a ruler; using measuring cups)
- Reading (looking at directions or reading a recipe)
- Following sequential directions
- Creativity and artistic sensibility
- Self-esteem and a sense of uniqueness
- Fine and gross motor skills
- Eye-hand coordination
- Cleaning skills (including responsibility)
- Fun!

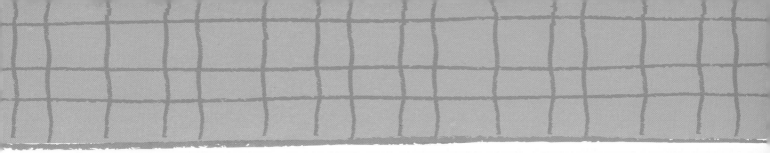

How to Use This Book

The crafts included here all require the supervision (and usually the hands-on help) of an adult, especially with preschool-aged children. However, each craft contains at least one "kids!" icon (featuring a *Sesame Street* character) indicating a step that your preschooler should be able to accomplish, depending on the skills and abilities of your individual child. Also included with each craft are special features written for the children that bring "words of wisdom" (or just fun thoughts!) from the *Sesame Street* friends.

The first step in creating each craft is to read through the directions for the project from beginning to end. That way you and your child will know what materials and tools you will need. If she is able, encourage her to read familiar numbers out loud from the materials list, and pick out her favorite letters of the alphabet. Although understanding written fractions can be difficult for preschoolers, you can certainly point out "½" in a materials list and explain the concept of "one half" by showing her that if you cut one whole pipe cleaner into two equal parts, you now have two halves.

Finally, although directions for these crafts are often quite specific in order to ensure clarity, remember that part of the fun of making crafts is to be creative. We encourage you to experiment with color, found objects, or decorating in any way that seems appropriate and appealing. Don't worry if the end result doesn't look exactly like the photo. Half the fun of crafting is developing your own style and expression.

A Few Thoughts on Safety

Avoid accidental choking. It's natural for very young children to put small objects, such as beads, magnets, and crayons, into their mouths. Please supervise your child, no matter what age, at all times. Make it very clear that none of these materials belong in the mouth, then keep a watchful eye.

Keep away from hot or sharp objects. When making your crafts in the kitchen, be sure you are working at a safe distance from a hot stove and sharp objects, such as knives.

Tie back long hair; roll up sleeves. Both you and your child should wear an apron, or old clothes, since they might get spattered with glue or paint.

Clean up before and after working with crafts. Start with a clean work surface so your materials will stay clean. After you've finished, clean up thoroughly.

Work slowly and carefully. Just do one step at a time.

GET CRAFTY

It's a good idea to keep all your craft materials together. You can design a special craft box, or purchase an inexpensive plastic container from an office supply or container store. Create a special craft workspace (if you have the space) and cover it with a plastic or paper tablecloth, newspaper, or other protection as you work.

Essential Tools

Here's a useful list of essential tools and materials you'll need to do most of the projects in this book.

- Scissors (those with rounded tips are safest for younger children)
- A set of acrylic paints in basic primary colors (red, blue, yellow, black and white)
- Paintbrushes in various sizes and thicknesses
- White glue and an old paintbrush to apply it
- Colored pencils; colored markers; crayons
- Black fine-tipped marker
- Pencils
- Ruler
- Large eraser

More useful materials

Here are some other materials you might want to have on hand. Look out for things to collect or interesting materials to store at home until you are ready to craft. This is a great way to reuse things and make less trash in the world.

Gift wrap

Recycled gift wrap can come in handy for many projects. If it's too crumpled, iron it with a cool iron, and it will be as good as new.

Cardboard

Use recycled cardboard from packing boxes, cereal boxes, laundry detergent boxes, or other cardboard packages to make your projects.

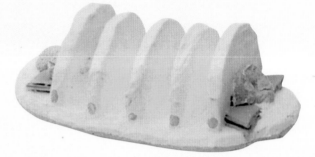

Fabric

Worn out blue jeans can be turned into bags, purses, and pencil cases. Scraps of patterned fabric can be used to make bean bags, pouches, as a coverings for boxes, or as decorations in infinite ways.

Odds and ends

Save odd buttons, earrings, and other old jewelry in cookie tins, then use them as craft decorations. Even old bottle caps (both metal and plastic) can be used in creative ways.

Objects from nature

When you are outdoors in the park or garden, pick up pretty leaves, interesting twigs, feathers, pinecones, seed heads, stones, and other objects from nature. At the beach, collect shells, pebbles, and driftwood.

TIPS FOR SUCCESS

Prepare your space

Cover your workspace with newspaper or a plastic or paper tablecloth. Make sure you and your children are wearing clothes (including shoes!) that you don't mind becoming spattered with food, paint, or glue. But relax! You'll never completely avoid mess; in fact, it's part of the fun!

Wash your hands

Wash your hands (and your child's hands) before starting a new project, and clean up as you go along. Clean hands make for clean crafts! Remember to wash your hands afterward, too, using soap and warm water to get off any of the remaining materials.

Follow steps carefully

Follow each step carefully, and in the sequence in which it appears. We've tested all the projects; we know they work, and we want them to work for you, too. Also, ask your children, if they are old enough, to read along with you as you work through the steps. For a younger child, you can direct her to look at the pictures on the page to try to guess what the next step is.

Measure precisely

If a project gives you measurements, use your ruler, T-square, measuring cups, or measuring spoons to make sure you measure as accurately as you can. Sometimes the success of the project may depend on it. Also, this is a great opportunity to teach measuring techniques to your child.

Be patient

You may need to wait while something bakes or leave paint, glue, or clay to dry, sometimes for a few hours or even overnight. Encourage your child to be patient as well; explain to her why she must wait, and, if possible, find ways to entertain her as you are waiting. For example you can show her how long you have to wait by pointing out the time on a clock.

Clean up

When you've finished your project, clean up any mess. Store all the materials together so that they are ready for the next time you want to craft. Ask your child to help.

SUNSHINE PLATE

YOU WILL NEED

- Old dinner plate with a wide rim
- Plastic wrap
- Newspaper squares
- White glue and brush
- Paintbrush
- Scissors
- Gold paint

1

KIDS

Cover the plate with plastic wrap, then use white glue to stick layers of newspaper squares all over it. Make sure the plate is completely covered.

2

KIDS

Leave the plate in a warm, airy place to dry. Then apply another layer of newspaper squares. You will need to do at least six layers to make the plate strong enough.

3

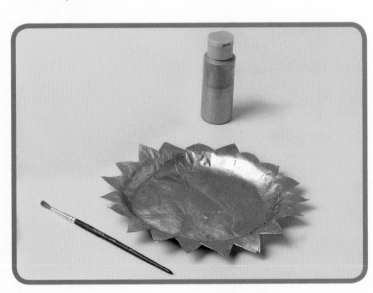

When the newspaper is completely dry, lift it off the plate and carefully peel away the plastic wrap. Cut a zigzag pattern around the edge of the plate.

4

Cover the plate with gold paint, and leave it to dry. Remember to paint both sides. You may need to do several coats to get a truly golden, sunshine finish.

DID YOU KNOW?
The sun is actually a star, just like those we see twinkling in the sky at night.

Decorate the edge of your plate with craft jewels to make it look like treasure!

SEASHELL MOBILES

YOU WILL NEED

- Seashells
- String
- Scissors
- Paintbrush
- Varnish
- Driftwood or branch

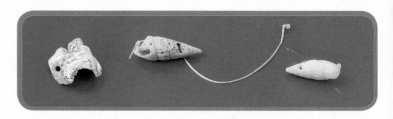

Thread the string through the first shell and tie a large knot underneath, to hold the shell in place. Find shells that already have holes in them, so you won't have to make them.

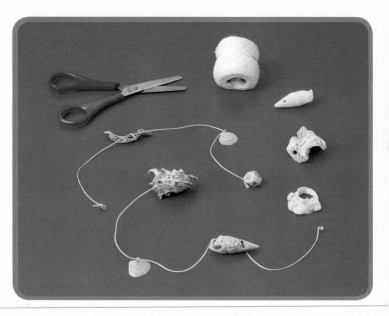

Continue threading on shells, tying a knot each time. Make as many separate shell strings as you like.

KIDS

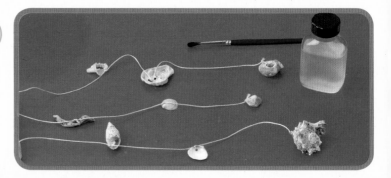

Varnish the shells and leave to dry.

4

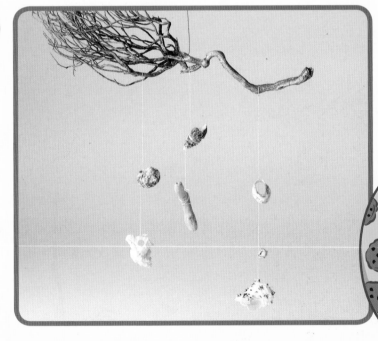

Make loops at the end of the shell strings to hang them from a piece of driftwood or a branch. Check the mobile for balance as you put them on.

5

Hang up your pretty seashell mobile where you can see it, to remind you of a happy vacation.

LEAF PICTURES

YOU WILL NEED

- Fall leaves (different shapes and sizes)
- Heavy book (e.g. dictionary)
- White glue
- Picture frame
- Paintbrush
- Acrylic paints: black, gold
- Sponge
- Saucer

1 KIDS

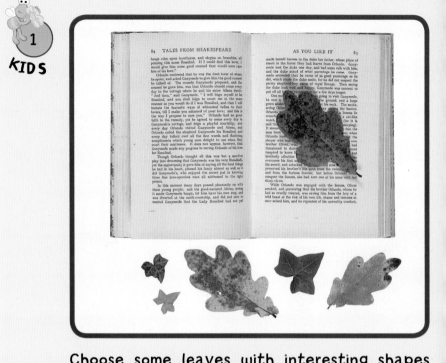

Choose some leaves with interesting shapes and colors. Place them between the pages of a heavy book. Leave them for several weeks to flatten and dry.

2
IDS

Arrange the dry leaves on a sheet of paper. Glue them down and ask an adult to put the paper in a frame.

3
IDS

To make an even more decorative picture, paint the leaves black. When dry, sponge on gold paint in patches and leave to dry.

DID YOU KNOW? The warm sunny fall days and cool fall nights make the red, orange, and yellow leaves appear even brighter.

Elmo makes leaf people. A leaf could be a body or a head. Then draw the rest of the picture around it.

PAPER SNOWFLAKES

YOU WILL NEED

- Small paper plate
- Pencil
- Scissors
- White glue and brush
- Glitter: silver, gold, white
- Thread

1

KIDS

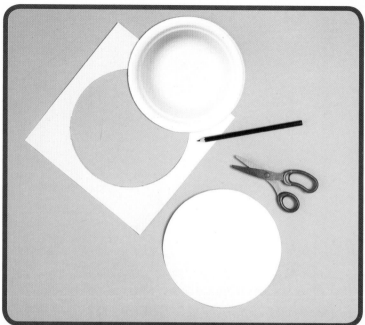

Trace around a small plate onto a piece of white paper. Cut out the circle.

②

Fold the circle in half three times, so you end up with a triangle shape. Draw a snowflake pattern along the folded edges of the triangle. Cut out the pattern, making sure you don't cut all the way through the folded edges.

Carefully unfold your snowflake. Cover one side with glue and sprinkle it all over with glitter. Shake off any loose glitter onto scrap paper, and keep it to use for the other side of your snowflake. Let dry.

④

Cover the other side of the snowflake in glue and glitter. When the glue and glitter are completely dry, tie some thread through a hole in the top to hang it up.

DID YOU KNOW?
No two snowflakes are exactly the same, but every real snowflake has six points.

Catch a snowflake on your tongue. It tickles!

NOTEPAPER

YOU WILL NEED

- Paper: blue, white, green
- Black marker
- Scissors
- White glue
- Hole punch

Decorate the blue sheet of paper first. Draw, then cut out, small fluffy white clouds and glue them onto the sky.

Decide how low the skyline will be, then draw and cut a wavy line across the top of a sheet of green paper to make hills. Glue the green paper on top of the blue to create a scene.

③

Make a snow scene decorated with a cheerful snowman. Draw a snowman on a white sheet of paper. Remember to draw the horizon, too. Use scissors to cut out the snowman and horizon, then glue the sheet of white paper onto the blue sky.

④

:IDS

Decorate the snowman using a black marker to make his face. Use a hole punch to make lots of tiny white circles for snowflakes, then stick them on your snowy scene.

FABRIC PRINTING

YOU WILL NEED

- Carrot, medium potato, apple
- Knife
- Kitchen towel
- Sponge
- Fabric paint: various colors
- Plain fabric
- Cookie cutters

1

Cut a carrot in half, longways. Use the sponge to spread a little fabric paint onto the flat side of the carrot.

2

KIDS

Gently press the carrot down onto the fabric. Do not move it about, or the paint will smudge. Print a row of carrots. Leave the printed fabric in a safe place to dry. Follow the directions that come with the fabric paint to set the dye.

3

Cut a potato in half. Press the cookie cutter firmly into the potato and cut away the potato around the outside. Remove the cutter, and pat the stamp dry with a kitchen towel, so it's ready for printing.

4

KIDS

Use a sponge to apply fabric paint to the stamp. Print your pattern.

5

Cut an apple in half and pat it dry with a kitchen towel.

Cut up the fabric into rectangles and print on them, to make place mats or napkins for all your family.

6

KIDS

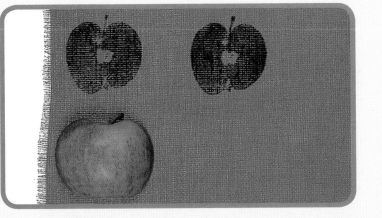

Use the sponge to apply fabric paint to the apple surface and press it down firmly onto the fabric.

DOGHOUSE AND PET

YOU WILL NEED

- Empty milk or juice carton
- Scissors
- Paint
- Paintbrush
- Oven-bake clay or plasticene
- Modeling tool
- Marker pen

KIDS

1

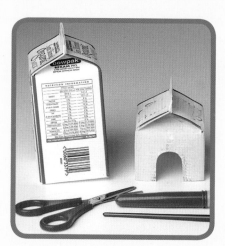

Cut the top off a clean empty carton. This will be the doghouse roof. Now cut a door in the front of the house for your pet.

2

Paint the house. It may need two coats. When it is dry you can write your pet's name above the doorway with a marker pen, if you want to.

3

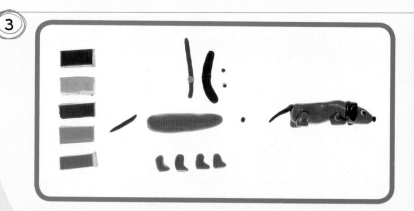

Make a pet out of modeling clay. Use the modeling tool to join the parts together. Bake it in the oven according to the manufacturer's instructions.

4

When it is completely cool, you can put your pet in his new home. To help him settle in, why not make him a food bowl and snacks out of bits of leftover clay?

DID YOU KNOW?
A dog's sense of smell is one thousand times better than a human's.

SHELL FRAMES

YOU WILL NEED

- Thin cardboard
- Scissors
- Grout
- Spatula
- Selection of shells
- Varnish
- Paintbrush
- Adhesive tape

①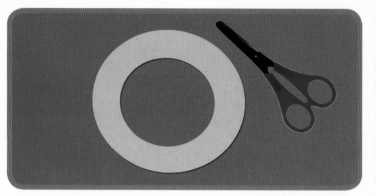

To make the frame, cut out a small circle from a piece of thin cardboard. Cut out a smaller hole out of the center. This will be the hole for your picture.

② KIDS

Apply a layer of grout around the frame using the spatula.

③ KIDS

Gently press in the shells in a fun pattern around the edge of the frame.

When the grout has dried, paint the shells with a layer of varnish.

5

Tape a photograph to the back of the frame with tape, so that the picture shows through the hole. Hang up the frame or use it as a small paperweight.

DID YOU KNOW?
Long ago, some people used shells as money!

Put one of your favorite beach photos in the frame, so the shells remind you of sunny days.

GIFT TAGS

YOU WILL NEED

- Thin, colored cardboard
- Colored construction paper
- Ruler
- Pencil
- Scissors
- Hole punch
- Gluestick
- Ribbon: red, green

Measure and cut out some cardboard rectangles six inches by four inches. Fold them in half to make tags, and press along the fold line. Punch holes in the corners, as shown.

Draw some Christmas decorations onto construction paper and cut them out. Use the hole punch to make lots of circles in different colors out of leftover bits of paper.

3
IDS

Glue the decorations and hole-punch circles onto the front of the folded tags. Thread ribbon through the holes, so you can attach your tags to gifts.

DID YOU KNOW?
Holidays are a great time to get in touch with friends and family.

A grown-up can help you write the name of someone special.

FRIDGE MAGNETS

YOU WILL NEED

- Oven–bake clay in a variety of colors
- Modeling tool
- Baking sheet
- Aluminum foil
- Magnets
- Strong white glue

1 KIDS

Knead the clay in your hand until it is soft enough to shape.

2 KIDS

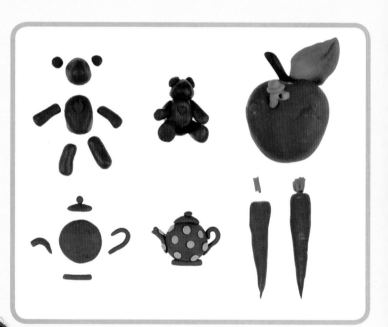

Experiment with the clay to make different items to decorate your fridge magnets. You could try making animals, faces, a teapot, fruits, or vegetables. You could even make a teddy bear from brown clay.

③

Press a magnet into the back of each clay item, then remove it before baking. Bake your objects in the oven, on a foil-covered baking sheet, following the manufacturer's instructions. Make sure you ask a grown-up for help. Once cool, glue the magnet in place.

DID YOU KNOW?
Magnets stick to anything made of, or containing, a metal called iron.

Elmo is going to make the letters of his name: ELMO.

POP-UP CARDS

YOU WILL NEED

- Colored thin cardboard
- Scissors
- Ruler
- White glue
- Colored paper
- Colored markers

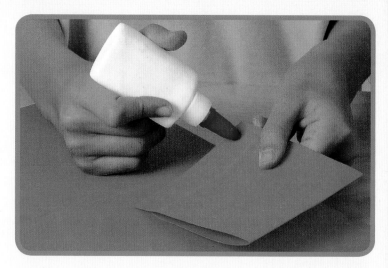

1 Fold a sheet of cardboard in half, then open it out. Now cut a smaller rectangle and fold in half. Fold a lip along the two shorter edges and glue them to the inside of the larger card to make the vase. Check the vase flattens when the card is shut.

2 Cut stems and leaves out of green paper, and glue them inside the vase. Cut out some paper flowers and glue them onto the stems, making sure they are hidden when the card is closed.

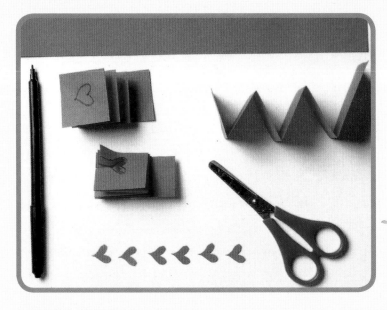

Cut lots of small hearts from folded red paper to decorate the vase.

4
DS

Decorate the front of the card with a large paper heart, then glue a smaller one in a contrasting color in the middle. Now you are ready to write your message inside the card.

DID YOU KNOW?
The heart that beats inside your body doesn't look at all like the heart shapes you see on Valentine's Day!

PINECONE BIRDS

YOU WILL NEED

- Clean, dry pinecones
- Acrylic paints
- Paintbrush
- Pipe cleaners
- Scissors
- White glue
- Two googly eyes
- Scrap of orange cardboard
- Colored feathers (from craft shop)
- Thread

1

KIDS

Paint a pinecone in a bright color and leave to dry. Twist a colorful pipe cleaner around the middle of the pinecone to make two legs the same length.

2

Cut another pipe cleaner into lengths, three inches long. Twist the pieces around the ends of the legs to make the bird's feet, as shown.

DID YOU KNOW? When wet weather is on the way, pinecones close up.

Cut a triangular beak out of a folded piece of orange cardboard. Glue on the googly eyes and the beak. Glue feathers into the side of the cone to make the wings.

4

Tie a loop of thread to the top of the pine cone, if you wish, and hang up your bird.

YOU WILL NEED

- Thick cardboard
- Scissors
- Paper
- Glue
- Ribbon
- Pretty pictures from magazines
- Photographs

1

You will need two equal-sized pieces of thick cardboard for the cover. Glue them onto colored paper, as shown, leaving a gap between them.

2

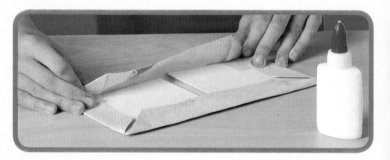

Fold in the colored paper neatly and firmly, then glue it down, so that the outer edges of the two pieces of cardboard are completely covered.

3

Take a long piece of colored paper and fold it back and forth as if you are making a fan. This will make the pages of the wallet.

4

Glue a piece of ribbon to the inside of both cardboard covers, down the middle, and leave to dry. This will tie in a bow to keep your wallet closed.

5

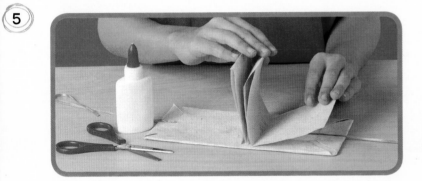

Glue one end of the folded page section to the inside front cover. It should cover the ribbon, too. Glue the other end to the inside back cover.

6

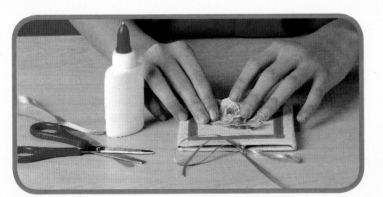

Decorate the front cover with ribbon and a picture of something pretty cut from a magazine.

DID YOU KNOW? Mother's Day is celebrated in many countries around the world.

Fill the wallet with photos of you and all your family.

DOOR HANGERS

YOU WILL NEED

- Colored cardboard 4 x 9 inches
- Pencil
- Ruler
- Scissors
- Foam letters
- Selection of colored paper
- White glue
- Colored markers (optional)

①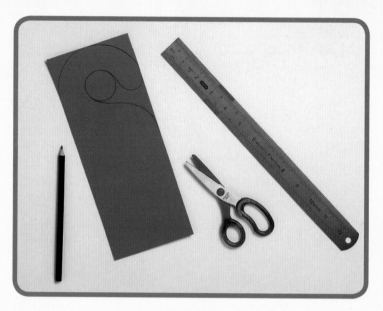

Draw a small circle near the top of the cardboard, as shown. Then draw a shape like the top of a letter "S" around the circle.

②

Carefully cut out the "S" shape with a pair of scissors, to make the basic door hanger. It is now ready to be decorated.

KEEP OUT

3

Use foam letters and glue to write a message on your door hanger. If you have no foam letters, write a message with colorful pens instead.

4

Decorate your door hanger with paper cut-outs. Look at these door hangers for ideas, then let your imagination go!

DID YOU KNOW? People hang all sorts of things on doors and doorknobs. Can you think of any?

You can decorate the other side, too!

FELT JEWELRY

YOU WILL NEED

- Felt squares: various colors
- Scissors
- Fabric glue
- Rubber band
- Needle and colored embroidery thread
- Polyester stuffing
- Ribbon

1

Cut three squares of colored felt, each slightly smaller than the last. Layer them, using a little glue to hold them in place.

2

Now roll the felt up tightly into a sausage, using glue to stick it. You will need to hold the sausage in place with a rubber band while the glue dries.

3

KIDS

When the glue is thoroughly dry, use scissors to cut the sausage into beads.

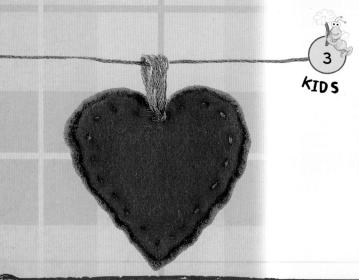

4

To make a heart pendant, use two squares of colored felt. Cut out a heart from each color, making one smaller than the other.

5

Place a little stuffing between the layers and sew them together with colored thread. Make a ribbon loop at the top for threading.

6

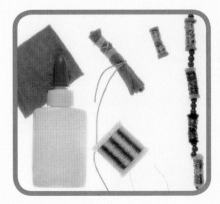

To make these beads, roll a small square of felt. Hold in place with glue, then wind colored thread around it to make decorative bands.

DID YOU KNOW? In some cultures, felt is used to make tents, rugs, shoes, and clothing.

GLASS PAINTING

YOU WILL NEED

- Clean, old glasses, jars, and bottles
- Black outliner
- Paintbrush
- Water-soluble glass paints

1

Before you begin, wash and dry the glass. Use the black outliner to draw a picture on the glass. Be sure there are no gaps for the glass paint to leak through.

2

KIDS

When the black outline is completely dry use the paints to fill in the color. Wash the brush well between colors, and dry it before dipping it into the next color. Let dry.

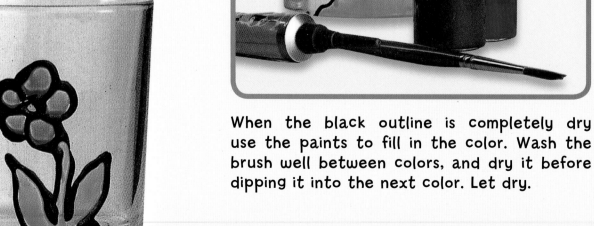

DID YOU KNOW? People throw away a lot of glass jars and bottles. Try recycling them instead!

Thank-you, Elmo. I'll put it in a pretty vase.

SEASIDE JEWELRY

YOU WILL NEED

- Seashells and pebbles
- Jewelry clasps
- Earring hooks
- Varnish
- Paintbrush
- Wire
- Thread
- Scissors

1

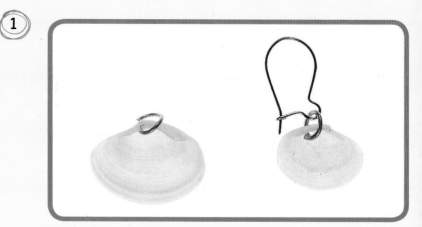

Some shells have tiny holes in them, but you can also use ready-made clasps from a craft shop to hold the shell in place. Attach an earring hook to each shell and you have a pretty pair of earrings.

2

KIDS

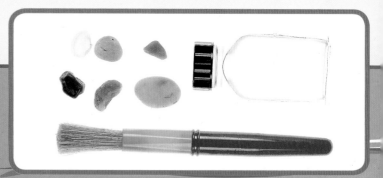

Find pebbles with interesting markings on them. Paint over them with clear varnish and leave to dry.

3

Wind a piece of wire around a pebble and make a loop at the top.

4

Attach a piece of thread to the loop and use this to hang your jewelry around your neck or wrist.

DID YOU KNOW?
If you hold a seashell to your ear, you can hear what sounds like waves on a seashore.

ORIGAMI BOX

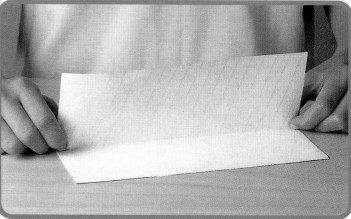

1

KIDS

Fold a rectangle of paper in half lengthwise.

2

KIDS

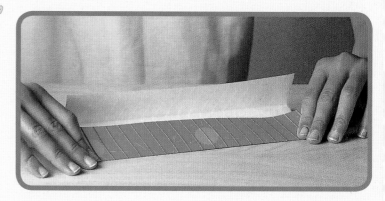

Fold each half into the middle so you have 4 equal sections.

3

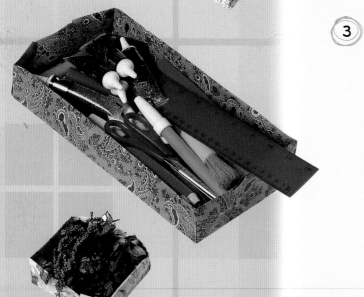

Make a narrow fold outward from both long edges.

④

Fold in the corners and tuck them under the small fold.

⑤

Place your fingers in the corners and carefully open out the box into shape. Use your fingers to make folds at the four corners.

⑥

LUNCHBOXES

YOU WILL NEED

- Plastic food storage box with lid or lunchbox
- Craft foam
- Scissors
- Foam letters
- White glue or sticky foam pads
- Double-sided tap (optional)

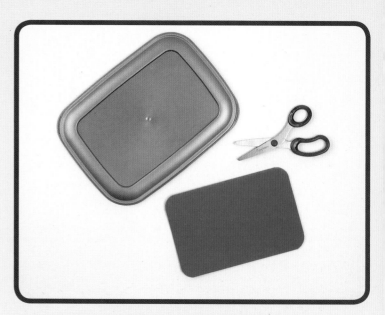

Cut out a rectangle of foam to fit onto the lunch box or lid of the plastic box. Round off the corners to make it look neat.

Cut out foam shapes to decorate the foam rectangle. Arrange them with some ready-cut foam letters to spell out your name. Experiment with positioning, until you are happy with your design, then glue it in place.

Place the finished design onto the lid. You can use glue, but if you use sticky foam pads or double-sided tape it can easily be removed for washing or switched for another design.

DID YOU KNOW? The world's biggest pre-packed sandwich was eight feet two inches long!

Cut out shapes of your favorite foods to decorate the lid.

MINI BUG POTS

YOU WILL NEED

- Air-drying clay
- Water
- Acrylic paints
- Paintbrushes
- White glue and brush
- Water-based varnish

①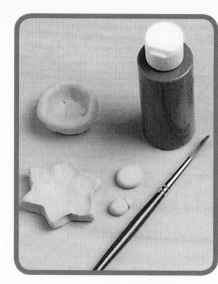

Push your thumbs into a ball of clay to make the pot shape, smoothing it with your fingers. Make a lid out of a flat disk of clay. Stretch it into a flower shape, then make a ladybug from a ball of clay.

2

KIDS

Paint the pot, lid and ladybug, allowing them to dry between colors. When completely dry, glue the bug to the lid. Apply a coat of varnish over the whole thing.

Experiment with different shaped pots and creepy crawlies. Let your imagination go!

DID YOU KNOW? There are more kinds of insects in the world than any other type of creature.

Oh, what a cute little bug!

PAPERWEIGHTS

YOU WILL NEED

- Pebbles
- Acrylic paints
- Paintbrushes
- Varnish

1
KIDS

Collect some interesting pebbles at the beach. Wash and dry them before you begin the craft.

2
KIDS

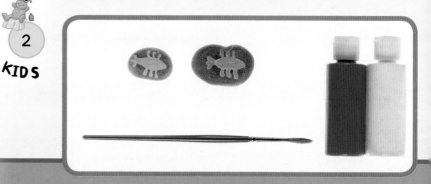

Use a fine paintbrush to paint on a pattern or picture.

3
KIDS

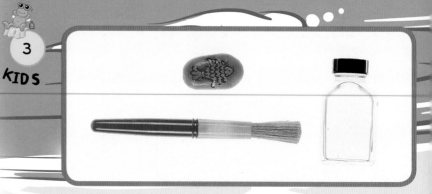

When the paint is dry, add a layer of varnish to protect the surface and give your paperweight a glossy finish. Let dry thoroughly before you use it.

DID YOU KNOW? Pebbles are smooth because they tumble and bang together in the sea, wearing the edges down.

53

YOU WILL NEED

- Thin cardboard 10 x 8 inches
- Colored markers
- Glitter
- White glue and brush
- Scissors
- Tissue paper (cut into thin strips)
- Colored paper (2 colors)
- Adhesive tape
- Two sticks

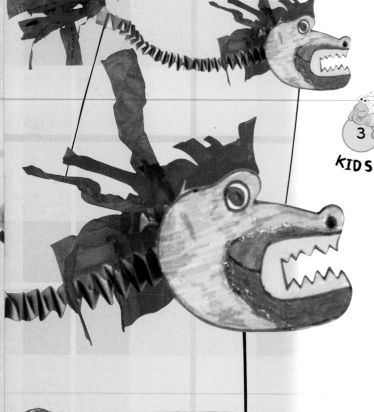

1

Draw a dragon's head onto thin cardboard. Use colored markers to color it in, then decorate it using glue and glitter.

2

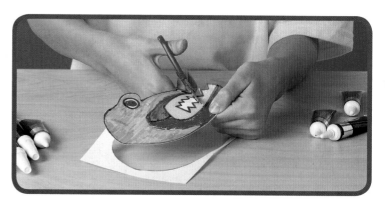

Carefully cut out the dragon's head.

3

KIDS

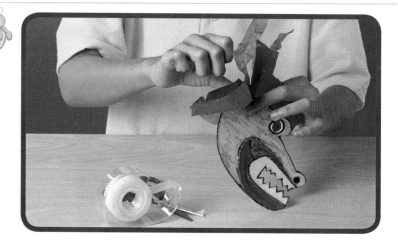

Tape half the strips of tissue paper to the back of the dragon's head.

(4)

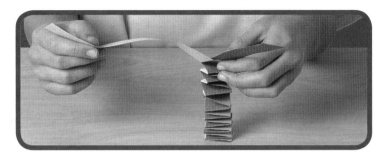

Cut two long, thin strips of colored paper the same length. Glue one to the other to make an "L" shape. Fold the yellow strip over the top of the pink strip and crease it. Then fold the pink strip down over the yellow. Continue until you can glue down the final fold.

5
KIDS

Glue the rest of the tissue paper to the dragon's tail. Glue the head to the other end of the body.

(6)

Use tape to attach the two sticks to the body – one at the head end, the other at the tail end.

DID YOU KNOW?
Chinese New Year is celebrated with a big parade. At the end of it, a dragon dances to the sound of drums, horns, and gongs!

Chinese New Year is a SUPER holiday!

ENVELOPES

YOU WILL NEED

- Occasion card: birthday, holidays, Valentine
- Colored paper
- Scissors
- Glue
- Colored markers

1 KIDS

Place your card in the center of the paper. Fold up the bottom of the sheet to cover the card completely. Leave an inch at the top, and ½ inch on each side.

2 KIDS

Fold the top flap down, over the card.

3

Open out the paper completely and fold in the sides over the card. Make sure the card fits easily the folded shape.

4

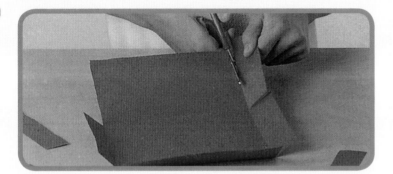

Trim the excess paper from the sides of the front flap using the folds to guide you. This will make it easier to close your envelope.

5

Cut in at angles on either side of the top flap to shape it.

6

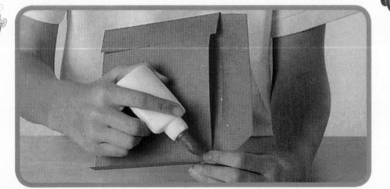

Use glue to hold the envelope's shape.

DID YOU KNOW? Zip codes are numbers after your address that help the Post Office deliver mail to the right house or building.

Elmo likes to decorate the envelope with markers or crayons.

PENCIL CASES

YOU WILL NEED

- Tall containers with tightly fitting lids, such as potato chip tubes
- Newspaper
- White glue and brush
- Scissors
- Acrylic paints
- Paintbrushes
- Glitter

Clean the container. Make sure your pens, pencils and ruler will fit inside. Glue on a layer of newspaper squares so the box is completely covered. Leave in a warm, airy spot to dry.

Place a sheet of paper under your craft before sprinkling the glitter. Pour any extra glitter back into the container.

Paint the pencil case with a base coat, let dry, then paint on any picture or pattern you like. You could add shiny stars or glitter for decoration.

SOCK PUPPETS

YOU WILL NEED

- Clean, old sock
- Thin cardboard strip
- Scissors
- Colored felt: pink and same color as sock
- White glue
- Big black button
- 2 small white felt circles
- 2 small black buttons
- Needle and thread
- Length ribbon

①

Push a long strip of card inside the sock, so that it is stretched out flat. This will make it easier to work with.

② KIDS

Cut out a long felt tongue. Dab glue at one end and stick it near the end of the sock, so it can flap about.

③

Turn the sock over. Sew on the big button for the nose. Sew or glue the small black buttons onto the white felt circles for eyes, then sew or glue them in place. Cut out two felt ears. Stick them in place, as shown.

④

KIDS

Leave the puppet to dry, then tie a ribbon around the neck and secure in place with glue. What will you name your puppet?

DID YOU KNOW? People have enjoyed puppet shows for over 2,500 years!

Try to use old, odd socks – and make sure you wash them first!

STENCIL TOY BOX

YOU WILL NEED

- Big box
- White glue and brush
- Old newspaper
- Acrylic paints and paintbrush
- 1 sheet white paper and pencil
- Scissors
- Sponge
- Small plate
- Adhesive tape

1 KIDS

Glue two layers of newspaper inside and outside the box, covering it completely. Do this in stages, allowing the box to dry in a warm, airy place between each layer.

2 KIDS

When the layers are completely dry, paint the box. You may need two or three coats of paint to cover the newspaper completely. Remember to let the paint dry between coats.

Draw a simple stencil design onto the center of a sheet of paper and cut it out. You may want to make a few stencils with different shapes.

Loosely tape the stencil to the side of the box. Dip the sponge in a little paint and pat it on the plate to get rid of any extra, then dab it over the stencil. Practice on scrap paper before decorating your toy box.

NAPKIN RINGS

YOU WILL NEED

- Cardboard tube
- Scissors
- Pencil or marker pen
- White glue and brush
- Tissue paper strips
- Foil candy wrappers torn into strips

①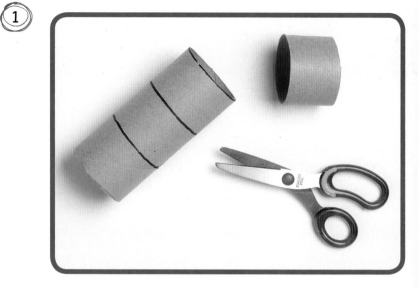

Mark sections about one inch wide on the cardboard tube, as shown, then carefully cut the tube into sections.

2 KIDS

Brush glue all over the outside and inside of each ring. Wrap tissue paper strips around them, brushing on more glue to help them stick. Glue foil strips over the tissue strips for a sparkly effect.

DID YOU KNOW?
Long ago, instead of using napkins, people wiped their hands on a slice of bread.

Touch up with glue in spots that need it, then leave to dry. Roll up a napkin and push it into a ring, then put at table setting.

Napkins are handy for sticky desserts!

PICTURE PUZZLES

YOU WILL NEED

- Picture you have drawn or one from a magazine
- Thin cardboard (same size as your picture)
- White glue
- Ruler
- Pencil
- Scissors

1 KIDS

Glue your picture onto a piece of thin cardboard, making sure every part of the picture—even the edges—is firmly glued down.

2

Divide the picture into evenly sized pieces with a pencil and ruler. Carefully cut the picture into pieces along the pencil lines.

Jumble up the pieces, then try to complete
your picture puzzle.

Keep all the puzzle pieces in an envelope
so they don't get lost.

DID YOU KNOW?
The biggest jigsaw
in the world is bigger
than a ping-pong
table and has over
18,000 pieces!

I bet you
are a SUPER
puzzle-doer!

IDENTITY TAGS

YOU WILL NEED

- Lid from a glass jar
- Colored cardboard
- Pencil
- Scissors
- White glue
- Craft foam
- Glitter glue
- Paper clip

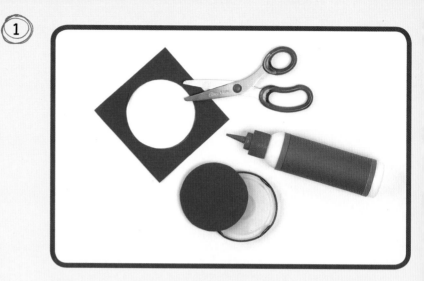

1

Draw around the jar lid onto cardboard to make two identical circles. Cut them out.

2

Glue one of the circles inside the lid. Put the other circle to one side. Cut out your initial from craft foam. Make sure it will fit inside the lid. Glue it in the middle of the lid, then add some glitter glue decoration. Leave to dry.

(3)

Bend open a paper clip and glue it to the back of the lid. Glue the second cardboard circle over the top, and leave it to dry.

4

KIDS

When your bag tag is completely dry, it is ready to hang from your bag.

DID YOU KNOW?
There are twenty six letters in the English alphabet! The Russian alphabet has thirty-three!

BOWLING

YOU WILL NEED

- 6 or 10 large empty plastic drink bottles
- Acrylic paints
- Paintbrushes
- Sand

1 KIDS

Carefully wash out the bottles. When they are completely dry, screw on the lids tightly.

2 KIDS

Give each container a colorful base coat. You may need to paint each one with two or more layers of paint to cover it completely. Leave to dry.

3 KIDS

Now it's time to decorate your bowling pins. Paint on patterns and shapes in different colors. When all your bottles are painted, decorated, and dry, they are ready to use.

DID YOU KNOW?
People have played bowling games since the days of ancient Egypt.

Stand the bottles in a triangle shape, as shown in the picture. If you are using six bottles, place one at the front, two in the middle, and three in the back row. Use a small ball to play your bowling game. If they are too easy to knock over, fill them with a little sand to make them heavier.

toys

PHOTO ALBUM

YOU WILL NEED

- Thin colored posterboard
- Scissors
- Hole punch
- Colored yarn or string
- Colored paper

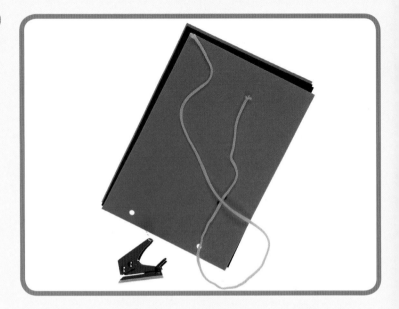

1

Cut two card rectangles for the front and back cover, and some paper pages for inside. Make two holes in the cover and pages, making sure they all line up.

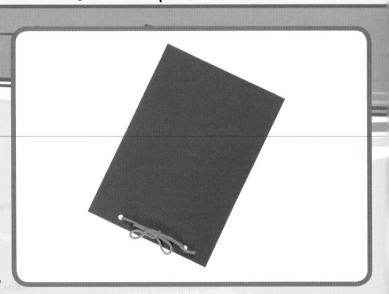

2

KIDS

Thread some colored yarn or string through the holes and tie a knot or bow to hold the album together.

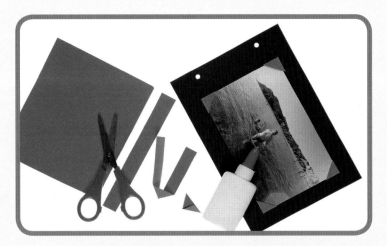

Cut a thin strip of paper. Fold it as shown to create a triangular "photo corner," cutting off the long extra bits of paper. Do this four times for each corner of your photo. Glue the back of each "corner" to stick the photo on a page.

Decorate the pages with colorful borders. Write the date, place, and who is in the photo, so you'll never forget.

④

IDS

Decorate the cover of your album with a picture or pattern. Then fill it up with your favorite photos.

MAGIC PICTURES

YOU WILL NEED

- Thin cardboard or paper: white
- Scissors
- Colored markers
- Clear plastic folder
- Adhesive tape

Take a sheet of thin cardboard or paper and fold it into three equal sections as shown in the picture.

2

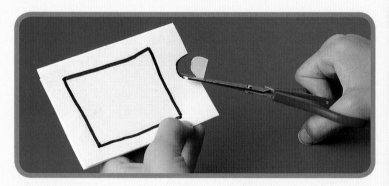

On the front flap mark out a rectangle and the finger grip space. Cut away the finger grip space.

3

Open out the cardboard and cut out the rectangle. This is the front frame of the card.

Decorate the front frame with a pattern. Cut a piece of paper the same size as one section of the card and draw on your design.

5

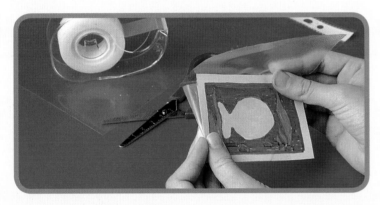

Slip your picture into the plastic folder with the top against a fold. Trim the plastic to fit the picture. Tape the back to the plastic.

6

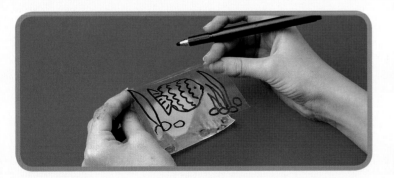

Use a black marker to draw an outline of the picture on the plastic.

7
KIDS

Open out the card, and slip the bottom flap between your picture and the plastic layer on top. The bottom flap is now between the two. Fold the frame down over the top. Grip the plastic and paper and pull; the picture will magically appear in color as you pull it out.

BOOKMARKS

YOU WILL NEED

- 2 x 6-inch long strips thin cardboard
- Pencil
- Scissors
- Colored marker pens

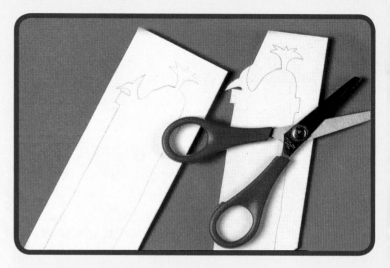

① This picture shows you how to make a whale bookmark, but you can choose any design you like. Use your pencil to outline a whale (or whatever design you choose) on top of a long rectangular shape. When you are happy with the shape cut it out.

2

IDS

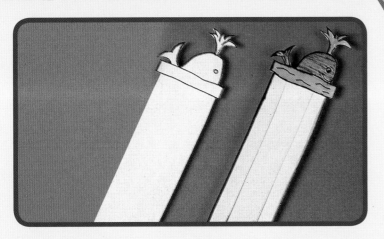

Use markers to color in the design, then carefully give it an outline with a black marker.

3

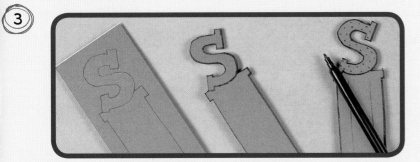

You can personalize your bookmark by using your initial. Draw it in pencil first. Give it an outline with a black marker when you decorate it.

4

This bookmark would look good in a gardening book.

DID YOU KNOW?
English has more words than most languages. And thousands of new words are added every year!

Mmm. Delicious!

AQUARIUM

YOU WILL NEED

- Large shoe box and lid
- Scissors
- Acrylic paints and paintbrush
- Sheet of plastic wrap (blue if available)
- White glue
- Advesive tape
- Green tissue paper
- Pebbles
- Thin cardboard and paper
- Colored markers
- Glitter
- Gold thread
- Self-adhesive stars (optional)

①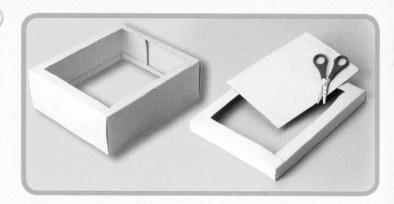

Cut a rectangle out of the box lid and the base of the box.

②

Paint the box and lid blue, inside and out.

③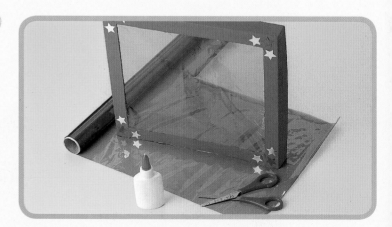

Glue a sheet of plastic wrap over the cut-out spaces.

4
KIDS

Cut tissue paper strips for the weeds. Tape them to the aquarium roof so they dangle down. Lay pebbles on the bottom.

5
KIDS

Draw fish on the thin cardboard and decorate them with paint and glitter.

6

Attach them to the roof with gold thread, then glue the lid on. Decorate with stars if you wish.

DID YOU KNOW?
Public aquariums can be enormous, with tanks the size of a football field!

YOU WILL NEED

- Large colored paper cup
- Scissors
- Colored paper
- Adhesive tape
- Colorful crêpe paper or tissue paper
- Two white cardboard circles
- Black marker pen
- Thread

1

Cut off the bottom of the paper cup. If the cup has writing on it, cover it with a piece of colored paper, secure it with tape or glue, and trim the edges.

2

KIDS

Cut out circles of colored paper, and use them to decorate the outside of the paper cup. Stick on two white circles for eyes, adding a black dot in the middle for the pupils.

3

IDS

DID YOU KNOW?
Which way is the wind blowing? Watch the streamers on your creature!

Cut or tear long strips of crêpe or tissue paper and tape them all the way round the inside of the cup, at the widest end.

4

Tape a long loop of thread at the top end of the cup so you can hang it up in the porch or on a tree. Watch the streamers dangle and blow in the wind!

TRINKET BOXES

YOU WILL NEED

- Corrugated cardboard from a grocery box
- Ruler
- Pencil
- Scissors
- Adhesive tape
- Old newspaper
- White glue
- Acrylic paint
- Paintbrushes
- Tissue paper

①

Measure and cut out two squares the same size for the box base and lid. Then measure four small rectangles for the box sides. Their longest edge should be slightly shorter than the sides of the base.

②

Use tape or glue to hold the box together. Use the top of the box to help you draw a small square to stick on the inside of the lid. Check that the lid fits into the box.

Glue two layers of newspaper squares over the box and lid. Check the lid still fits, then leave in a warm airy place to dry.

When the newspaper is dry, paint a base coat of color. You may need to paint a second coat to cover them completely. When dry, decorate the box and lid any way you wish.

DID YOU KNOW?
Real gemstones are found underground. They are dug up, then cut and polished to make them shine.

Scrunch up tissue paper and put it inside your box, before you put trinkets in it.

PUMPKIN FUN!

YOU WILL NEED

- Pumpkin (any size)
- Black marker pen
- Knife
- Tealight

1 **KIDS** Use a black marker pen to draw a face onto one side of your pumpkin. You can draw triangles for the eyes and nose, and a jagged strip for the mouth, if you like.

2 Ask an adult to cut a circle around the top of the pumpkin for the lid, and the holes for the eyes, nose, and mouth.

3 Place a tealight inside the pumpkin so it can shine through the holes. Ask a grown-up to light it for you.

DID YOU KNOW? Halloween is a holiday celebrated each year on October 31. Children dress up in costumes for fun and get treats.

Remember to say "thank you" each time you get a Halloween treat!

SCENTED CHARMS

YOU WILL NEED

- 2 cups flour
- 1 cup salt
- 1 cup water
- Large bowl
- Wooden spoon
- Rolling pin
- Shaped cookie cutters
- Baking sheet
- 1 drinking straw
- Acrylic paints and paintbrush
- Sweet-smelling essential oil (e.g. lavender)

1

To make the dough, place the flour, salt, and water in a large bowl. Stir the mixture until it forms a dough. Remove from the bowl and knead for five minutes.

2
KIDS

Roll out the dough on a lightly floured surface and cut out any shapes you like with the cookie cutters.

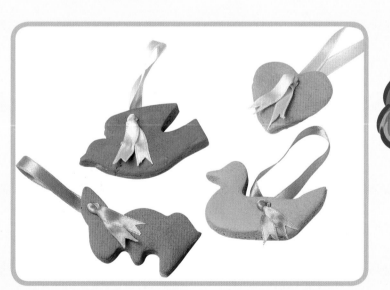

Place them on a greased baking sheet. Poke a hole in each shape with the end of a drinking straw. With a grown-up's help, bake the shapes in the oven at 265°F, for four hours. Let cool.

4

IDS

Paint the shapes on both sides, leaving an area on the back unpainted. Drip a few drops of essential oil onto this patch, to give the charm its fragrance.

5

Push a length of ribbon through the hole. Tie a knot and hang the charm in the window or on the wall.

DID YOU KNOW?
Even doctors have sometimes used sweet-smelling oils to make people feel better.

MOSAIC MATS

YOU WILL NEED

- Sheet white paper
- Ruler
- Pencil
- Colored paper
- Scissors
- White glue
- Clear contact paper

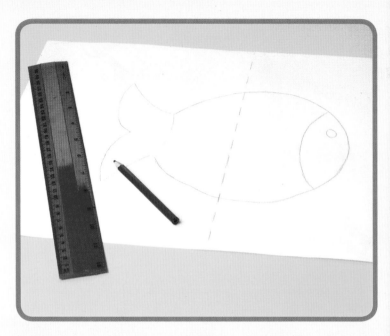

Begin by drawing a simple outline of a fish, or anything else, on your paper. Make sure that the picture is in the middle.

Decide which colors you want for your picture, then use a ruler and pencil to measure out lots of small squares on colored paper. Cut them out. Make sure you have plenty of each color.

DID YOU KNOW?
The ancient Romans, used tiny mosaic tiles to make wonderful pictures on floors and walls.

Elmo made place mats for Elmo's whole family to use at dinnertime!

Glue the squares onto your picture. Begin in the top corner, and work from one side to the other.

4

Your finished mosaic should look something like this. To protect it, ask a grown-up to cover it with a layer of clear contact paper.

PARTY HATS

YOU WILL NEED

- Thin cardboard
- Scissors
- Crêpe paper
- Needle and thread
- Glue
- Colored paper
- Glitter
- Pencil and ruler

Cut a band of card about three inches wide, to fit around your head with a small overlap.

Cut a strip of crêpe paper, the same length as the band but deeper. Hand baste a line of loose stitches along the long side of the crêpe paper.

3
KIDS

Glue the crêpe paper onto the band, with the basting at the top.

Glue the two ends of the hat band together. Pull the ends of the thread to gather the paper. Tie a knot.

5
KIDS

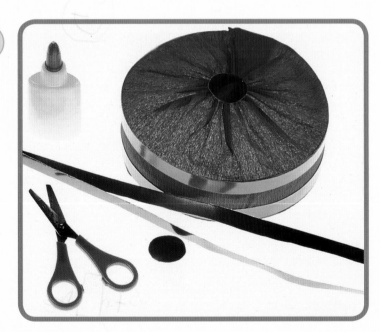

Cut out a small circle of card or paper and glue it over the center of the hat. Decorate the hat with colored paper, card, and glitter.

DID YOU KNOW?
We lose lots of body heat through our heads – so hats are good for keeping us warm.

Use glitter, sequins, colored gems, and bright ribbon to decorate your hats.

ANIMAL CLIPS

YOU WILL NEED

- Thin cardboard
- Pencil
- Scissors
- Marker pens: red, yellow
- Eraser
- White glue and brush
- Clothespins

1

KIDS

Carefully draw the outline of an animal's head on the cardboard with a pencil.

2

KIDS

When you are happy with your animal design, color it in using colored markers.

Then draw a dark outline around the colored animal. Cut out your animal and glue it onto a clothespin. Now it is ready to hold your notes!

DID YOU KNOW? An adult lion's roar can be heard up to five miles away. ROARRR!

If you want, glue the clip onto a magnet and put it on the fridge.

INDEX